Poems Of Faith, Love And Compassion

By Elaine Coltham

Poems of Faith, Love and Compassion
Copyright © 2000 Lainee Matloch Publications
Reprint 2001

All rights reserved. Written permission must be secured from the publisher to use or reproduce any part of this book, except for brief quotations in printed reviews or articles.

Published by Lainee Matloch Publications
Ipswich, Suffolk. IP3 0QP

Illustrations: Georgina Coltham,
Peter Coltham, Elizabeth Coltham
James Coltham

Printed by ByWord Books, Suffolk

Scriptures quoted from The Youth Bible, New Century Version (Anglicised Edition) copyright 1983 by Nelson Ward Ltd.
9 Holden Avenue, Bletchley, Milton Keynes.
MK1 1QR

ISBN: 0-9538176-1-X

Cover Illustration by Georgina Coltham

Contents

Foreword
by Bishop Richard

Introduction - Acknowledgements - Dedication

Words of Faith
'Pebble on the Beach' - 'The Journey' - 'Searching ...'
'I Reflect On You' - 'For You' - 'Lord I Look Upon ...'
'I Heard ...' - 'Earth's Resurrection' - 'Lord, Grant me Silence'

Words of Love
'Dusky Eyes' - 'Little One – James' 'Lizzie'

Words of Compassion
'Brother-man' - 'Old Man on Second Bench'
'Prayer for Kosovo' - 'Diana'

And Lastly, For The Children
'Today on my Swing' - 'The Sandcastle'

List of Illustrations

Foreword
By the Bishop of St Edmundsbury & Ipswich

We live in an age when the media can bring us face to face with horrors from around the world whether they are the result of natural causes or the brutality of human beings. Even the mass media knows that there is a saturation point and the plight of different peoples around the world can vanish from the headlines as rapidly as they originally appeared.

People react in different ways to what they see and each of us knows the feeling of saturation and the way in which the next horror becomes one too much and we switch off in our minds or quite literally switch off the radio or television.

Elaine Coltham has refused to switch off and has turned her reactions into a mixture of poetry and prayer. The one merges into the other in the pieces in this book and I commend them to you as a way of responding.

+Richard St Edmundsbury & Ipswich

Introduction

This book is the culmination of many years of writing poems and then placing them in the bottom of a drawer where some had remained forgotten over time.

I have always had a great love of writing and have for many years found it helpful to express through poetry my feelings about some of those things which touch, or disturb, us all.

After much encouragement from family and friends, I decided to gather some of my poems with others I have written this year, and publish them in the hope they will strike a chord with the reader. The result is a collection of poetry written about some of the most important aspects of my life.

In Faith, Love and Compassion, every poem has a brief introduction to set the scene of my thoughts and provide some background to the inspiration behind each one. If my words do strike a chord occasionally as you read, then this book will have achieved its main objective.

If you have bought this book, I would like to thank you on behalf of Tear Fund and East Anglia's Children's Hospices, to which organisations all profits are donated.

Thank you

To my family for their inspiration, encouragement and, most importantly, love.

To Bishop Richard for writing the foreword.

To Ann and Anne for believing I could self publish.

To Mum and Ray.

To Geoff and Hope.

And,
To You for buying this book

Dedication

For Peter, Georgina, James,
Elizabeth, and my dear parents,
with much love.

Words of Faith

As Paul Wrote
"I pray that Christ will live in your hearts by faith and that your lives will be strong and built on love."

Ephesians 3
V 17.

By Elaine Coltham

Pebble on the Beach

As you will discover in this book, I have received much inspiration from being close to the sea. For this poem, I had a picture of how God's love is like a tide flowing over us. I imagined each of us as being a pebble on life's huge beach. This feeling came to mind again this year when I was staying at Sizewell Christian Conference Centre. It was wonderful to hear the sea lapping the shore outside and to be surrounded by so many people full of love and praise for our Father God.

Pebble on the Beach

I was at the cross-roads of my life,
Looking for the pathway to your door.
You shone your light on me that day,
No need to stumble any more.

And I know you are my father,
And you gave Jesus for me.
With your ever loving glory,
You have set my spirit free.

I'm but a pebble on life's beach,
Please cleanse me with your flowing tide.
And give me courage, strength and faith,
I'll never wander from your side.

And I know you are my father,
And you gave Jesus for me.
With your ever loving glory,
You have set my spirit free.

(1996)

By Elaine Coltham

The Journey

My inspiration to write this came when thinking about two special events coming up at church on the following day.
Firstly a friend was going away to work abroad and, secondly, a baby was going to be baptised.
Both were to embark on a journey. My friend was travelling many hundreds of miles to a new country to work. The little girl would also begin a journey which, although it would not at this time involve travelling, would help her grow in the knowledge of Jesus' precious love.

The Journey

My life is but a journey
And I know that it will be,
Much stronger and fulfilled
If I take my rest with Thee.

The paths may not be easy,
The roads not always straight.
But Jesus, with your constant love,
I can pass through any gate.

Though many miles I travel,
Crossing countries, sea and land.
I will carry the love of Jesus
Wearing His armour wherever I may stand.

And I will grow upon that journey
Searching for others as I go.
Like the disciples on their travels,
Seeds of your love I must sow.

May I learn as each day passes
So every precious moment shall be
A celebration of a life's journey with You,
And beyond, in eternity.

(2000)

By Elaine Coltham

Searching

During many happy seaside holidays our children have made it a family mission to find amongst the pebbles and debris a precious stone - a piece of amber. I think we have lost count of all the times we have been convinced, "This one must be it."

Thinking back at the end of one such day I realised we are so often searching and looking for more. This poem was inspired not only by our searches along the seashore but by realising that when we find Jesus we have found a jewel so precious in our life that we need to search no more.

Searching...

Like a child on a pebble filled beach
Looking for precious stones to find
    Still searching
    - Searching for more.

Like a scientist on a voyage of discovery
Enquiring answers of our creation and being
    Still searching
    - Searching for more.

Like an intrepid climber reaching up
Scaling unclimbed peaks, new challenges
    Still searching
    - Searching for more

Like an athlete running with pounding heart
For new records to break, medals to win
    Still searching
    - Searching for more.

Like a theologian reading and tracing
Events in the bible, looking for meanings
    Still searching
    - Searching for more.

Like a child Dear Jesus when you found me
I discovered your vast love and forgiveness
    Searching no more
    - Searching no more.

(2000)

By Elaine Coltham

I Reflect on You

One morning, sitting on my garden bench in the warm sunshine encircled by the shade of a leafy arch, I was thinking about all the places we can go to reflect on God. I had a picture in my mind of all the places near and far from home where we can consider His vast love for us.

I Reflect On You

Under an arbour of leaves
Where the dappled shadows play
I reflect on You
In the heat of the day.

By some distant shore
Where the waves lap the sands
I consider your vast majesty
And the beauty You planned.

From a mountain high
Where the hills and valleys meet
I gaze on Your creation
So perfect and complete.

In the stillness of night
Where only darkness I see
I praise You My Lord
That You know and care for me.

(2000)

By Elaine Coltham

For You

I had been thinking about the sheer vastness of God's wonderful creation. This poem orbited around my head in the early hours of one summer night as I considered the most amazing detail our Creator planned for us.
I hope that God will forgive me for imagining and writing the words I thought that He must often feel about the provisions that He has given so freely for us all.

For You

My love immeasurably overflows
For You
My earth I created with an intrinsic balance
For You
My light I have shone through the darkness
At You
My sky has made the horizons
For You
My hands have thrown clusters of stars into space
Over You
My seas, land and skies breathe with creatures
Near You
My rest I have given as a restorer
For You
My planet, all I asked was a caretaker
Of You
My sorrow at your greed painfully weeps
For You
My forgiveness like the rainbow shines
Over You
My only dear Son I sent to die
For You
My longing for you to accept me as Father
To You
My door stands wide open, I wait silently
For You
My promise will always be there
For You
My love Immeasurably overflows .... For You.

(2000)

By Elaine Coltham

Lord, I look upon ......

This was written for a church service on the theme of 'light'. I was trying to capture the brilliance of light and draw a parallel with Luke's Gospel account of Jesus teaching us to place our lamp in the open so it may shine for others to see.

Lord I Look Upon...

Lord I look upon the brilliance of your creation,
As I gaze at the flecks of dawn's light,
Etched across the dying night sky,
I see the hope of a new morning.
The sun rising, as you Lord rose from the tomb.
And as you banish the darkness,
Your light envelopes me, bathes me in forgiveness.
I feel your love surrounding me, holding me,
Filling me with a flame to burn for you.
So let me be your beacon shining on a hillside,
A light placed out in the open,
Shining for everyone to see.
A flame burning with compassion,
Enlightening darkest corners,
Warming coldest hearts,
Breathing your love through my small flame.

(2000)

By Elaine Coltham

I Heard.........

With the dawn of the new millennium and all the excitement and celebrations I wrote these words to focus on what I as a Christian felt I was celebrating. Whilst listening to our rather ancient church bell being rung on the first day of 2000 I was reminded again of Jesus and the impact He had on earth during His relatively short life. I wanted to tell His story in this poem from humble birth to cruel death on the cross. The poem ends with what I would hope for this millennium the chance for peace and reconciliation through Jesus with the assurance that His love remains for you and me always.

"And I will be with you always, even to the end of this age."
Matthew 28 v 4.

I Heard ...

I heard about a baby
Born two thousand years before now
In Bethlehem's little stable
Near oxen, sheep and cow

I heard about a star
Guiding kings from far-off lands.
And shepherds on a hillside –
Did they really understand?

I heard about King Herod –
His palace and his might.
But he feared the little baby –
Tried to extinguish this new light.

I heard they called him Jesus
He was God's only son
His purpose already told to us –
prophets knew Him to be the One

I heard He healed the sick
Turned water into wine.
And, sending Him to live on earth
God showed to us a sign

I heard He preached forgiveness
No sin too big for Him
But, though we were the victors
On earth He could never win.

I heard about a cross
A man nailed and left to die.
Surely this wasn't my Jesus,
reigning now on high.

By Elaine Coltham

I heard He came to save me.
I cried, and felt ashamed.
He lived and walked among us
All the time anticipating His pain.

I heard that He waits patiently
To be invited in.
How could I have ignored Him?
He bled and died for my sin.

I heard Him when He knocked
I flung wide my own heart's door.
Seeing for myself God's precious love
I could want for nothing more.

I heard the church bells ringing
To mark two thousand years
Since Jesus came among us
To take away our fears.

I heard the world is searching
For Peace and Reconciliation.
Let us listen out for Jesus –
He cries out to every nation.

(2000)

By Elaine Coltham

Earth's Resurrection

In the midst of a cold, grey winter it seems hard to imagine that the soil will bring forth new life. The disciples must have felt immense bleakness when Jesus was killed, and could not believe that resurrected life would have been possible. This poem was inspired by a tiny shoot - the 'against all odds' sign - which reminds us that the earth's resurrection always faithfully comes again.

Earth's Resurrection

From the shroud of winter
Rises a miracle.
From cold barren earth
Comes the shoot of new life.

Triumphant in arrival
Leaving the death of winter, grieving
Spring heralds, for us, new beginnings.
Earth's resurrection comes again.

Not just with our eyes
Can we witness this transition
Our ears delight and rejoice
In resplendent chorus of early morn.

Thank you everloving God
That your unfailing renewal
Brings new life and fresh hope
And darkness always followed by dawn.

(2000)

By Elaine Coltham

Lord, grant me silence

Lord, grant me silence
To listen to you
Lord, give me wisdom
In all that I do
Help me show compassion
To all who I meet
Lord, throughout my life
Be your hands and your feet
Lord wash me with peace
When the storms break the shore
Live deep in my heart Lord
For today and evermore.

(2000)

By Elaine Coltham

Words of Love

"Love is patient and kind. Love is not jealous, it does not boast and is not proud. Love is not rude or selfish, and does not get upset with others. Love does not count up wrongs that have been done. Love is not happy with evil but is happy with the truth. Love patiently accepts all things. It always trusts, always hopes, and always remains strong. Love never ends."

1 Corinthians
v 4 - beg. of v 8.

By Elaine Coltham

Dusky Eyes

This poem was written for Georgina our first child. She was born with such beautiful dark eyes and the sheer exhilaration of being a mother to this lovely little girl was all the inspiration that was needed to write this poem dedicated to her.

Dusky Eyes

Dusky Eyes, I love you
Let my arms surround you
You are all I long for
All that I adore.

Dusky Eyes, I need you
Need you safe beside me
To see me through each new day
With your gentle ways.

You have made me someone
Someone with something special
The gift of love and laughter
To share with you always

Dusky Eyes, don't ever leave me
Without you I'm nothing
Like a flower without the sun and rain
A bird with broken wings.

Dusky Eyes, I want you
We belong together
Our love has climbed a mountain
And reached the highest peaks.

Dusky Eyes, I love you
Let my arms surround you
You are all I long for
All that I adore.

(1981)

By Elaine Coltham

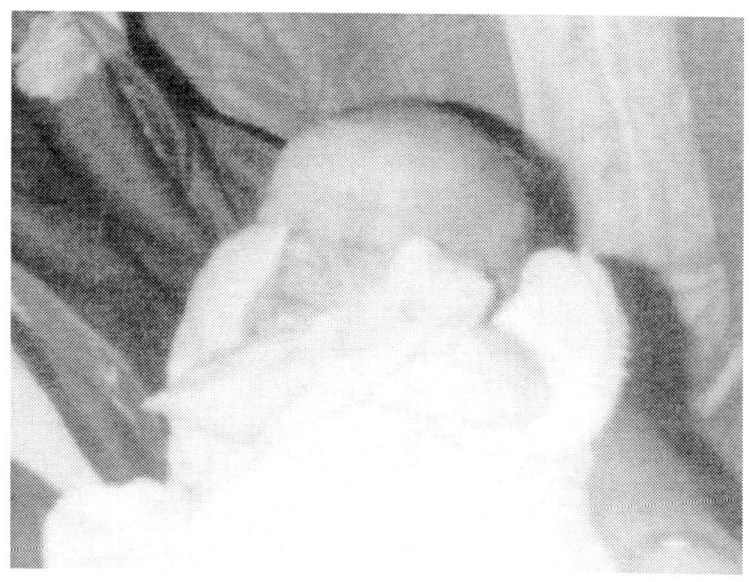

Little One - James

Our son was born at 1.30 in the morning. In the stillness of the night, looking at him peacefully sleeping, I was thinking of all the months of anticipation when waiting for a new baby to be born. I wrote this poem with the memories of that night, in the following year when our sleepless nights had subsided!!

Little One - James

Little one so tiny
With soft and downy hair
Blinking eyes in the sudden light
Skin so delicate and fair.

For months I've longed to hold you
And through the months we've grown
To an intimate love and understanding
Of the greatest bond ever known.

Your precious life just beginning
And my joy that you are here little one
This new day is dawning - I'm so happy
For we have just welcomed our son.

(1981)

By Elaine Coltham

Lizzie

This little poem, although it has few words, paints an exact picture of our youngest daughter, and I think anyone who knows her will agree.

Lizzie

Sparkling Eyes
Cheeky grin
Heart full of love
So now we begin.

Lizzie is mischief
Lizzie is cheer
She is the light
That shines through our year.

Lizzie is laughter
Abounding with fun
In her is a sparkle
As bright as the sun.

(2000)

By Elaine Coltham

Words of Compassion

"Listen, my dear brothers and sisters! God chose the poor in the world to be rich with faith and to receive the kingdom God promised to those who love Him."

James 1
Chapter 2 v.5

By Elaine Coltham

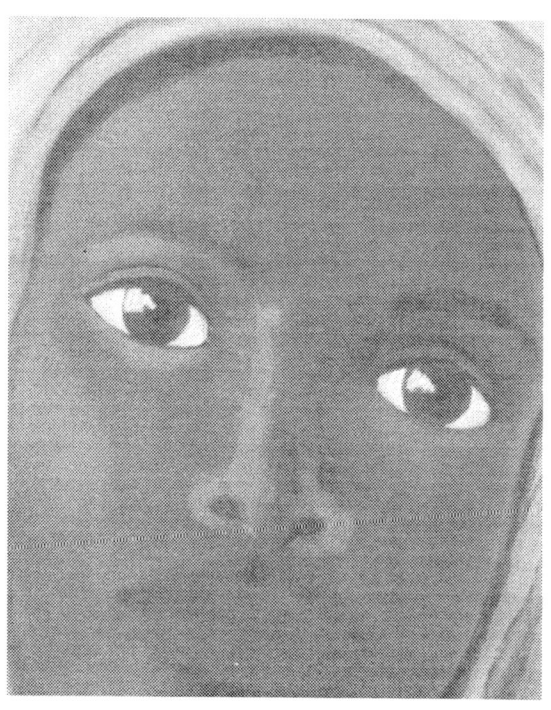

Brother-man

I wrote this poem in 1981 at the time of a tragic famine in Ethiopia. Nineteen years later as I write this introduction, the struggle for survival in this area continues. For our fellow brothers and sisters there is still much help needed.

Brother-man

You know you are my Brother-man
But you're so far away
Our tongues speak of different words
Your night is my day.

I read about your heartache
See your shadowed face on my T.V.
Compassion burns within me
I wonder how your suffering can be.

Is there no hope for your children?
Will they live past one year old?
So how many more must die
Before your plight to us is sold?

Western society complains of obesity
The need to lose so much weight
But you could survive my brothers
With what is left each day on our plates.

Because we should all be equal
For that's the way we were made
Jesus died for everyone
So you and I could be saved.

Oh yes you are my Brother-man
Only a life-span away
When our tongues will speak together
On that everlasting day.

(1981)

By Elaine Coltham

Old Man on Second Bench

This poem sadly acknowledges the growing numbers of homeless people who can be seen in cities and towns, where a bench has become a bed, carrier bags a cupboard, newspapers a blanket and an overhanging tree a shelter.

Old Man on Second Bench

Old man on second bench
Biding time, watching, waiting
Why are you there?

Possessions roughly bundled
Bag ripping, contents spilling
Why do we just stare?

Clothes torn, stomach rumbling
Hunger gnawing, weakness spreading
Why don't we care?

Furrowed brow, sunken eyes
Discarded bottles dripping
Where is my prayer?

Night encroaches, coldness envelopes
We hurry past, ignoring
How do we dare?

Sunrise follows, morning beckons
Old Man on second bench
Are you still there?

(2000)

By Elaine Coltham

Prayer for Kosovo

In the spring of 1999 the media coverage showing the plight of thousands fleeing their homeland through fear of persecution touched my, and many millions of other hearts world-wide. This poem was written to recognise their suffering and to serve to remind me that these and other refugees ought never be forgotten.

Prayer for Kosovo

Tearstained little face
Years not unfolded yet
Tangible scars of sadness
A day they will never forget

Land of barren dust
Human ashes fall
People move on and on
Homelands blazing, broken walls

Women huddle, children cry
The voices of men are few
Carts pulled along forsaken roads
To a refugee camp queue

Sea of tents, cold grey dawn
A chill of fear in the air
Sparse possessions, most lost in the flight
Left behind in a house burning bare

Watching, waiting in a no-man's land
Will those hands ever touch again?
Wanting to wake, know this was a dream
Finding beside them their beloved men

Stories of hope, dashed by discoveries
Remembering only yesterday?
Shadowed faces where suffering is etched
Bow heads together to pray.

"Hear them O our Father
Turn cold hearts from stone
Comfort, heal and protect them
May they never feel alone.

By Elaine Coltham

Restore them to their homelands
Make straight and safe their way
Free the captive, touch the sick
Give them courage each new day.

From the ashes of their hatred
May tomorrow's dawn become
A new beginning for tolerance
A clean slate for everyone.

Melt away all bitterness
For generations to come
Let there be universal forgiveness
As You showed to us through Your Son."

(1999)

Diana

When Princess Diana died there was so much sadness. For many, she was an incredible figure who symbolised compassion and brightness. This poem was my small tribute to her memory.

Diana

New hope, bright star
Reaching out across the divides.

New compassion, bright star
Touching hearts and changing lives.

Eclipsed love, bright star
Hidden now by the darkness of death.

But rejoice! Bright star
Your light will continue – it will not die.

New home, bright star
In perfect peace shining for ever more.

New legacy, bright star
For a world to abide in tolerance and love.

And tomorrow, bright star
Your memory will encourage us on.

For you, bright star
The tears still flow, the flowers fade.
Our love remains for the star now saved.

(1997)

By Elaine Coltham

And Lastly... For the Children

Jesus said
" Let the little children come to me. Don't stop them because the Kingdom of Heaven belongs to people who are like these children."

Matthew 19
v.14

One thing uniting us all throughout the world is that we are, or have been, children. The next two poems I wrote with memories of childhood. They are very different from the other poems but I wanted to include them in this book as it was published to help those in need, especially children.

By Elaine Coltham

Today on my swing

I tried to capture within this poem the journey on a garden swing. The sights, smells and sensations experienced on the amazing flight, finishing with the anticipation of a continued journey to places you could only glimpse in your dreams.

Today on my swing

Today on my swing
I glimpsed the sun
I felt its warmth
The day had begun.

Today on my swing
I smelled the blossom sweet
As I brushed the lilac
With soaring feet.

Today on my swing
I spied tops of trees
Where black crow's nests
Swayed in the breeze.

Today on my swing
I touched the sky
I stroked a cloud
As it floated by.

Tonight on my swing
I will kiss the stars
As I glide past the moon
On my way to Mars.

(2000)

By Elaine Coltham

The Sandcastle

Trips and holidays at the seaside and, for me, memories of wonderful times spent in Cornwall as a small child.
Many years later the joy of taking our own children back to those same beaches of pale golden sand. The vastness of the sea with its' unpredictable power and endless hours spent making sandcastles, that would be taken away at the change of a tide.....

The Sandcastle

I built it with my mum
On our first holiday
It stood there proud and tall
For the rest of that day.

We went home for our tea
I sleepily went to bed
With visions of castle turrets
Floating around my head.

I awoke the next morning
Quickly ran to the beach
There was too much sand
The sea was out of reach.

I found the little shells
That bejewelled the castle wall
Then the lolly-stick drawbridge
But that was all.

I sensed my Mum behind me
She gently took my hand
We ambled up the beach again
She seemed to understand.

I built it with my Mum
On our first holiday
It stood there in the moonlight
Until the sea took it away.

(2000)

By Elaine Coltham

List of Illustrations

Front Cover Original acrylic painting by Georgina Coltham
'Pebble on the Beach' Photograph by Elaine Coltham
'The Journey' Photograph by Peter Coltham
'Searching' Photograph by Peter Coltham
'I Reflect on you' Photograph by Peter Coltham
'For you' Photograph by Peter Coltham
'Lord I Look Upon...' Photograph by Peter Coltham
'I Heard...' Original drawing by Georgina Coltham
'I Heard...' Original acrylic painting by Georgina Coltham
'Earth's Resurrection' Original drawing by Elizabeth Coltham
'Lord Grant me Silence' Photograph by Elaine Coltham
'Words of Love' Original painting by Georgina Coltham
'Dusky Eyes' Original drawing by Peter Coltham
'Little One (James)' Photograph by Peter Coltham
'Lizzie' Photograph by Elaine Coltham
'Words of Compassion' Original machine embroidery by Georgina Coltham
'Brotherman' Original painting by Georgina Coltham
'Old Man on Second Bench' Photograph by James Coltham
'Prayer for Kosovo' Photograph by James Coltham
'Diana' Original drawing by Georgina Coltham
'Today on My Swing' Photographic sketch by James Coltham
'The Sandcastle' Original drawing by Elizabeth Coltham
Back Cover Original silk painting by Elizabeth Coltham